Hajj
made
simple

Edited by
Saniyasnain Khan

Goodword

Research: Mohd. Harun Rashid
Art Editor: Mohd. Noman Khan
Managing Editor: Maria Khan

The chapters, the Spirit of Hajj,
the Message of Hajj, and Hajj: The Journey of a Lifetime
are based on *Haqeeqat-e-Hajj*
by Maulana Wahiduddin Khan

First published 2011
© Goodword Books 2011

Goodword Books
1, Nizamuddin West Market
New Delhi-110 013
email: info@goodwordbooks.com

see our complete catalogue at

www.goodwordbooks.com
www.goodword.net

Picture credits:
Najwah A. Marafie (cover, p. 10-11, 12-13, 45, pull-out
chart), Omar Chatriwala (p. 16-17, 44-45, pull-out chart),
Ali (p. 33, 35, 37, 45, 46-47, 48-49, pull-out chart),
Haris Abdulla (pull-out chart),
Bedouin Travel (p. 16), Hasham Malik (p. 17),
Rest of the images used
under license from 123rf.com

Printed in India

Contents

The Importance of Hajj 4

The Spirit of Hajj 6

The Message of Hajj 10

Hajj: The Journey of a Lifetime 14

Conditions for the Obligation of Hajj 18

The Etiquette of Hajj 19

Types of Hajj 20

Miqats, or Points at which Ihram is Assumed 22

Ihram 24

Ihram Garments for Men 26

Ihram Garments for Women 26

Prohibitions in the State of Ihram 27

Calling out the Talbiya 29

Tawaf al-Qudum or Tawaf of Arrival 30

The Station of Abraham 32

Sa'i or Brisk Walk 34

Departure for Mina 36

Departure for Arafat 36

Leaving for Muzdalifah 38

The Day of Sacrifice 40

The Manner of Ramy, or Stoning the Jamarahs, 42
    on the Days of Tashreeq

Tawaf al-Wada' or the Farewell Tawaf 43

Hajj: Round up 44

A Visit to the City of Madinah 48

Hajj on behalf of the Deceased or a Sick Person 51

The Prayers of Hajj 52

Some Prayers from the Quran and the Hadith 58

The Importance of Hajj

Hajj is the fifth pillar of Islam. It is incumbent only upon those Muslims who have the ability to undertake it. It has to be performed only once in a lifetime. However, one who has the ability to perform it more than once may perform it as many times as he likes. These additional performances will be counted as voluntary ones.

There are many sayings of the Prophet which show hajj to be an act bringing great reward and being held in high regard. The following are some of his sayings:

- The reward of a hajj *mabrur* (accepted hajj) is nothing less than paradise.

  Hajj *mabrur* means the hajj which is performed purely to seek God's pleasure in accordance with the *Sunnah* of the Prophet, committing no sin or other obscene acts, as is made clear by another saying of the Prophet:

  "Whoever performs hajj only for God's sake and does not indulge in sex or in evil deeds or sins will return (after hajj) as pure as the day his mother bore him."

- One who dies on his way to hajj will rise on the Day of Judgment in *ihram*, calling *talbiyah* (*Allahumma labbayka...*).

Why does hajj have such a great reward? The reason is that hajj, in fact, is symbolic of total submission and humbleness before the Almighty God. Leaving all his relatives, a pilgrim is drawn towards the House of God (Kabah), aroused by sentiments of pure love of the Almighty God. These sentiments of love and submission are demonstrated in various forms: in the form of circumambulation *(tawaf)*, brisk walking *(sa'i)*, kissing the black stone, offering prayers at different places and occasions, throwing pebbles at Jamarahs (*ramy*), the shaving of heads and the slaughtering of an animal, etc. All these rites show a pilgrim's total submission and utter humility.

The Spirit of Hajj

Hajj may be defined as a rehearsal for purposeful living such as was demonstrated by Ibrahim when he fulfilled the divine mission 4000 years ago. Living a purposeful life, he set an ideal example for posterity. The stages that Ibrahim had to go through in the process are symbolically observed by a pilgrim. During a specified period, a pilgrim re-enacts the historic events of Ibrahim's life, thus renewing his zeal to emulate him. He will reflect in his living what Ibrahim had done in his time.

The rituals of hajj are, in reality, the different stages of this purposeful kind of life. What one has to go through, having opted for such a life, had already been experienced in totality by Ibrahim. In every age, the faithful have to repeat the entire ritual in order to live a similar life. The true pilgrim is one who performs the rites of hajj with this intention, and experiences such sentiments.

A purposeful life demands first of all, a conscientious decision. This is outwardly reflected in the pilgrim's resolve to perform the prescribed rituals clothed in *ihram* (unstitched plain white garments). Another prerequisite is the expenditure of money for God's cause. A pilgrim reflects upon this when he spends his honestly earned money on the journey he undertakes.

A sense of purpose implies a focal point around which one's life is to be arranged. A pilgrim prepares himself for this by circumambulating the Kabah, for a life such as Ibrahim led necessitates constant activity. A pilgrim covers the distances between Safa and Marwah at a quickened pace to demonstrate his willingness for active participation.

A man with a purpose willingly sacrifices whatever is necessary to attain his goal. A pilgrim shows such willingness by sacrificing an animal. A man with a purpose also allies himself with men who have a common cause in order to make his actions stronger and more effective. A pilgrim on the Plain of Arafat demonstrates along with others the same feeling of unity and solidarity. But this is not the end. It is just the beginning. It begins in the places of hajj and completes its cycle with the return of the pilgrim to the activities of his day-to-day existence. Ibrahim's vision was one of *dawah* and reform. His was a divine mission, to which he devoted his whole life. Hajj, in fact, is neither more nor less than the resolve to revive the *Sunnah* of Ibrahim. The true pilgrim is one who returns from his pilgrimage filled with this resolve and having the appropriate sentiments.

The journey to perform hajj is a journey to God. It represents the ultimate closeness to God one can achieve while living in this world. Other acts of worship are ways of remembering God; hajj is a way of reaching Him. Generally we worship Him on an

unseen level; during hajj, we worship Him as if we are seeing Him face to face. When a pilgrim stands before the Kabah it seems to him that he is standing before God Himself. He is then moved to revolve around the Lord's house, like a butterfly encircling a flower, clinging to His doorstep like a slave begging for his master's mercy.

Among all Muslim acts of worship, hajj holds a prominent position. In one hadith, the Prophet called it the supreme act of worship. But it is not just the rites of pilgrimage that constitute this importance: it is the spirit in which hajj is performed. Let us put this another way and say that it is not merely a matter of going to Makkah and returning. There is much more to hajj than that, hajj has been prescribed so that it may inspire us with new religious fervour. To return from hajj with one's faith in God strengthened and rekindled – that is the hallmark of a true pilgrim. Hajj only takes its place as a supreme act of worship when it is undertaken in its true spirit, and performed in the proper manner. It will then be the greatest act in a pilgrim's life: he will never be the same again.

To perform hajj is to meet God. When the pilgrim reaches *miqat*, the border of the sacred territory, he is filled with awe of God: he feels that he is leaving his own world, and entering that of God. Now he is touching the Lord, revolving around Him, running towards Him, journeying on his behalf, making a sacrifice in His name, smiting His enemies, praying to the Lord and seeing his prayer answered.

The house of God in Makkah is one of God's signs on earth. There, souls which have strayed from the Lord take comfort in Him once again; hearts which have become hard as stone are brought low before Almighty God; eyes which have lost their vision are filled with divine radiance. But these blessings of hajj are available only to those who come prepared for them. Otherwise, hajj will be just a tour, a visit which leaves no lasting impression upon the one who makes it. This is the spirit of hajj which must be kept alive by the pilgrims.

The Message of Hajj

One special aspect of hajj is that it makes people remember God's scheme of things, which was first made known in Abraham's day, and fulfilled in the days of the Prophet Muhammad.

The rites of pilgrimage represent different stages of this scheme. Just as Abraham left his native land, Iraq, for Hijaz, the pilgrims leave their homes and depart for the Holy Land. Nearing Makkah they exchange their tailored clothes for two unstitched sheets like the simple cloths worn by the Prophets Abraham and Ishmael. When they reach Makkah, they walk around the House of God. Just as Abraham and Ishmael had done to solemnize their covenant with God.

Then pilgrims perform *sa'i*, which means walking seven times between the hills of Safa and Marwah in memory of Abraham's wife, Hajar's search for water. At Mina, Abraham, ready to sacrifice his son at God's command, was allowed by God to sacrifice a ram instead. Then, just as Abraham had thrown stones at Satan, who tried to thwart God's will, the pilgrims throw stones at three pillars, the Jamarahs. All throughout, they keep saying, "Here I am at your service, Lord."

The assembly of all the pilgrims on the plain of Arafat is spiritually the high point of the pilgrimage. Here, they all promise God to model their lives on the example set by Abraham, Hajar and Ishmael, doing God's bidding, whatever it may be, basing their lives on truth and, if necessary, giving up life's comforts and pleasures. God will be their focus, a goal from which they will never be diverted by the forces of evil.

When a man leaves his home and country to go on such a pilgrimage, he brims over with all the emotions aroused by the thought that he is embarking on a course which will lead him directly to God. He is, in effect, sloughing off his own world, leaving it behind him, and reaching out for the world of the Almighty. He is on his way to the House of God, a place where the great deeds of God's messengers and his followers have been preserved for all eternity; where we find the hallowed impressions of the lives of those who lived and died for the cause of God.

When the time nears for his entrance into the Haram (sacred territory), every pilgrim divests himself of his clothing in order to don a new kind of uniform – an unstitched plain, white garments which serve to heighten his consciousness of entering a new world. The very act of shedding his normal clothes (and with them all signs of status and ethnicity) signifies that he is separating himself from the way of life peculiar to his environment, and is now ready to become suffused with such emotions as are desired by God. In this way, thousands of men, in casting off their own hues, take on the hue of the Almighty. After clothing himself in *ihram* (godly raiment), the pilgrim finds his tongue of itself beginning to utter godly words – '*Labbaika Allahumma labbaika*! Here I am, O God, here I am!'

Labbaik (here I am) does not mean just that the pilgrim has come to stay in Makkah. It means that in leaving his normal abode, he has cast aside his whole way of life. It means, "I am ready to obey You." While on their pilgrimage, pilgrims simply give utterance to the word *labbaik*, but when they return to their own countries, they must put it into practice in their everyday lives.

On reaching Makkah, the pilgrim must perform *tawaf* (circumambulation). To do this, he enters the house of God, the great mosque in whose spacious central courtyard stands the Kabah, which was erected by the Prophet Abraham in ancient times. Then he goes round the Kabah seven times to demonstrate his willingness to make God the pivot of his whole existence.

After the *tawaf*, there comes the ritual of *sa'i*, which entails brisk walking from the hill of Safa to the hill of Marwah and back again. This procedure is repeated seven times in symbolic enactment of a promise, or covenant, to expand all of one's energies in the path of God. The form which this ritual takes can be traced back to the Prophet Abraham's wife Hajar, running from one hill to another in a frantic search for water for her young baby when they first arrived there.

The most important period of worship during hajj is the day-long sojourn on the plain of

Arafat. It is indeed, an awesome spectacle, with people from all over the world, clad in identical, simple, white garments, chanting, "Lord, I am present, Lord, I am present." This serves to impress upon the mind of the pilgrim how great a gathering there will be in the presence of God on the last Day of Reckoning. Once he becomes aware of the true significance of this, all his problems fall into their true perspective, and his life cannot but take a turn for the better.

Another practice during hajj is the casting of stones at Jamarahs. This is a symbolic act through which the pilgrim renews his determination to drive Satan away from him. In this way, he makes it plain that his relationship with Satan is one of enmity and combat. The next step for the pilgrim is to turn this piece of symbolism into reality, so that he may be purged of all evils, for all the evils besetting man are there at the instigation of Satan.

After this, the pilgrim sacrifices an animal to God, an act symbolizing the sacrifice of the self. In making such a sacrifice, the pilgrim indicates his willingness to forsake everything for God. His faith is such that if it comes to giving his life – the last thing that he would normally be ready to part with – he will not hesitate to do so in the service of God.

Hajj: The Journey of a Lifetime

About 5000 years ago the Prophet Abraham was ordered by God to lay the foundations of the Kabah – the House of God in Makkah – and to call people to make a pilgrimage to this House: "Exhort all men to make the pilgrimage. They shall come to you on foot and on the backs of swift camels; they shall come from every deep ravine."

Today, responding to the call of Abraham and following in the footsteps of the Prophet Muhammad, over two million people from every corner of the globe gather at Makkah to perform their hajj. Along with the profession of faith, daily prayers, a month-long annual fast and charity to the poor, hajj is one of the five tenets of Islam.

Hajj is a once-in-a-lifetime obligation for every Muslim, male or female, provided he or she is healthy enough to travel and has the means to undertake the pilgrimage.

The hajj period lasts from the 8th to the 13th of the Islamic month of Dhul Hijjah, and as the pilgrims arrive in Makkah, they are lodged in hotels and houses.

One very important obligation during hajj is the wearing of unstitched clothing comprised of two sheets (women wear normal clothes with a scarf to cover the head). All pilgrims, rich and poor, black and white, are dressed in this way, so that all men of all countries look alike in identical, simple garments, and no pilgrim may feel tempted to take pride of place over another.

At the Sacred Mosque of Makkah, the pilgrims encircle the holy Kabah seven times, which symbolically represents how man's life must revolve around God. Near the Kabah, are two small hills called Safa and Marwah. The pilgrims walk briskly back and forth seven times between these hills, a distance of about 394 meters. This rite is performed in memory of Abraham's wife, Hajar, who ran helplessly between the two hills seven times in search of water for her baby, Ishmael, who was suffering from thirst. God was pleased and sent an angel to dig a well from which the baby could drink water. The well, known as Zamzam, still quenches pilgrims' thirst.

On the first day of hajj, the pilgrims set out for Mina, which is a small town about 3 miles from Makkah. Here the pilgrims stay three nights and three days. The town, which normally has no more than a few hundred inhabitants, bursts into life on the days of

hajj, whenever two million people pour in to settle in tents to perform the rites of stoning the pillars that represent the devil. It is the place where, in obedience to God's commandment, Abraham took his son Ishmael to sacrifice

him. At that very moment, Satan appeared here to tempt Abraham to disobey God's command. But he threw pebbles at Satan to drive him away. So did young Ishmael and his mother. God was pleased with Abraham's response and sent an angel with a ram to be sacrificed instead of Ishmael. In commemoration of this act, Muslims sacrifice an animal on the Eidul

Azha. Today three pillars stand on the very spot where the incident took place. As one of the rites of hajj, the pilgrims also throw small pebbles at these stone pillars, which symbolize the Devil within ourselves. This is meant to kill the soul's desires and the ego.

From Mina, the pilgrims go on to Arafat, where the climax of the pilgrimage—"the standing at Arafat" takes place. For this reason the Prophet said, "Arafat is hajj." The centre of attention is the 200 feet high Mount of Mercy from which the last

Prophet preached his last sermon in 632 A.D. Seated on a camel, he addressed a crowd of 140,000, laying emphasis on the importance Islam attaches to human equality, regardless of social distinctions, the equal sharing of rights and duties by husband and wife, and the prohibition of usury, etc. Again, speaking with equal emphasis, the Prophet said: "No Arab is superior to a non-Arab and no non-Arab is superior to an Arab. No black man is superior to a red man and no red man is superior to a black man, except through *taqwa* (fear of God). Indeed the noblest among you is the one who is deeply conscious of God."

Here the pilgrims stand "before God", praying and listening to sermons. Everyone invokes God in his own way: standing or sitting, motionless, going on foot, or mounted. After a short stay here the pilgrims return to Mina via Muzdalifa. After staying again in Mina for two nights, they return to Makkah for the last *tawaf* of the Kabah, which ends the hajj.

Madinah, where the last Prophet's mosque and grave are situated, also attracts pilgrims in great numbers. Though it is not part of hajj, the pilgrims, out of their great reverence for the Prophet, stay there for a few days also, praying in the Prophet's mosque and visiting historical sites.

Conditions for the Obligation of Hajj

Hajj becomes obligatory for a person only when he is an adult of sound mind, he is financially able to undertake the journey, (he should be also in a position to maintain his independence during the period of his journey), he is physically fit enough to undertake the journey, and the route is safe for him (if the route is unsafe, hajj will not be obligatory for him). If the pilgrim is a woman, she should have a *muhrim* (a relative whose marriage to her is forbidden, such as, her father, son, brother, etc.) to accompany her (if she does not have such a relative, hajj will not be obligatory for her.)

Note: Hajj is not obligatory for children. It is permissible for them to perform hajj. However if a child performs his hajj in childhood, he will have to perform it again when he attains the age of maturity and hajj becomes compulsory for him. If he is very young, the formalities of hajj can be carried out by his guardian or parents. The parents will receive the reward of his hajj. During the Farewell Pilgrimage journey a lady once brought her child before the Prophet and enquired whether her child's hajj was valid. The Prophet replied, 'Yes, and you will receive a reward as well.'

The Etiquette of Hajj

When one who has fulfilled the conditions of the obligation of hajj and intends to set out on his holy journey, he should observe the following points of etiquette:

- Avoidance of indecency and sinful acts like abuse, obscene talk, quarrels, etc.

- Respecting fellow pilgrims and overlooking their faults

- Helping and co-operating with each other

- Keeping engaged in prayer and remembrance of God

- Bearing patiently any anger shown or provocation by other pilgrims

- Looking after the elderly and women pilgrims

Types of Hajj

There are three types of hajj. So the pilgrims should make sure what type of hajj they are going to perform. The details of each of them are as follows:

Ifrad: This is the simplest form of hajj. In this form of hajj the pilgrims enter into the state of *ihram* with intention of hajj only saying *"Labbayka bi hajjin"*, which means, "O Allah, I am here, at Your service, with hajj." After completing the rites of hajj, the pilgrims are released from *ihram*. For such a pilgrim, the sacrifice of an animal is not compulsory. However, he may perform umrah after hajj, if he so wishes.

Qiran: In this form of hajj, both hajj and umrah are performed in one *ihram*. The pilgrims assume *ihram* with the intention of performing umrah and hajj together, saying, "*Labbayka bi hajjin wa umrah.*" This means "O Allah, I am here, at Your service with hajj and umrah." Such pilgrims cannot take off their *ihram* garments after umrah; it is compulsory for them to first sacrifice an animal and perform *tawaf ifadah*.

Tamattu': In this form of hajj, the pilgrims enter into the state of *ihram* with the intention of performing umrah only, saying "*Labbayka bi umrah*" which means "O Allah! I am here, at Your service with umrah." Pilgrims performing this type of hajj, on reaching Makkah perform *tawaf* and *sa'i*, shave their heads or shorten their hair and remove *ihram,* thereby completing their umrah. Then they are free from all restrictions of *ihram.* They then again enter the state of *ihram* for the second time on the 8th of Dhul-Hijjah with the intention of performing hajj.

Of these three forms of hajj, *tamattu'* is better for those pilgimrs who do not bring a sacrificial animal along with them.

As for those pilgrims who bring a sacrificial animal with them, they should make known the intention of umrah and hajj together (i.e. the *qiran* form of hajj) and not remove *ihram* until sacrificing their animals on the 10th of Dhul-Hijjah. But those who have not brought sacrificial animals with them should make known the intention of umrah and hajj separately (i.e. *tamattu'* form of hajj). The Prophet himself performed hajj of the *qiran* type, as he had taken a sacrificial animal with him.

In both the forms, it is compulsory for the pilgrims to slaughter the sacrificial animal on the 10th of Dhul-Hijjah.

Miqats, or Points at which Ihram is Assumed

Miqats are specific places located at some distance from Makkah where the pilgrims intending to perform hajj or umrah, and coming from different directions, are required to assume *ihram*. They are not allowed to pass beyond these boundaries without entering into the state of *ihram*. The details of these places are as follows:

* Dhul Hulayfah: This is the *miqat* for those coming from Madinah. About 450 km. from Makkah, it is the farthest away of all.

* Al-Juhfa: This is the *miqat* for pilgrims coming from Syria, Egypt and other places in that direction. It is situated about 185 km. north-west of Makkah.

* Dhatul Irq: This is the *miqat* for pilgrims coming from Iraq, Iran and other places in that direction. It is situated about 94 km. north-east of Makkah.

* Yalamlam: This is the *miqat* for pilgrims coming from Yemen and the south. This *miqat* is situated about 54 km. south-west of Makkah. Of all the *miqats,* it is the nearest to Makkah.

* Qarn al-Manazil: This is the *miqat* for pilgrims coming from Najd and other Gulf countries. It is situated about 95 km. east of Makkah. This *miqat* is presently known as Sayl al Kabeer.

It is incumbent upon all pilgrims to assume *ihram* upon reaching their particular *miqat*. However, for those pilgrims who travel by plane, there is no harm if they wear their *ihram* garments before boarding the plane. Still, they should keep in mind that they must state their intention and call out *talbiyah* only upon reaching the *miqat*.

It is not proper for a pilgrim to delay in assuming *ihram*. If anyone enters Makkah without doing so, he must return to the nearest *miqat* and put on *ihram* there and then enter Makkah. In case of his failing to do so, a ransom (i.e. a sacrifice of an animal like goat or sheep etc.) will be due from him.

Those who live within the *miqat* area should assume their *ihram* at home. But this will not apply to those coming in from areas outside the *miqat* with the intention of performing hajj or umrah. They should assume *ihram* at the *miqat* itself.

Those travelling by plane can assume *ihram* at Jeddah airport.

Ihram

Ihram is the primary requirement of hajj or umrah. One cannot start performing the rites of hajj or umrah without having entered into the state of *ihram*.

Before putting on *ihram* garments, the pilgrims should trim their nails, remove unwanted hair, take a full bath and then wear the wrappings of *ihram* in such a way that one piece is tied around the waist and the other thrown over the shoulder. The male pilgrims can use perfume. Then they should state the intention in their hearts about the hajj or umrah they are going to perform. If the intention is only to peform hajj, they should say *"Labbayka bi hajjin"*, which means "Here I am, at Your service with hajj." If the intention is only to perform umrah, they should say *"Labbayka bi umrah"*, which means, "Here I am, at Your service, with umrah." And for hajj and umrah together as in the case of pilgrims performing the *qiran* type of hajj they should make their intention known by saying, *"Labbayka bi hajjin wa umrah."* This means, "Here I am at Your service with hajj and umrah."

It is better if the intention of *ihram* is made known

Ihram is the name for the particular clothing pilgrims wear. But from the Prophet's time ihram has meant more than that; wearing it is a sign of the special way pilgrims live while they are on hajj.

Each pilgrim rids himself of his selfishness, and the petty jealousies and concerns of ordinary life, and dedicates himself to prayer and worship of Allah. He feels truly sorry for his sins, and seeks God's forgiveness. He lives as simply as possible, and promises in his heart to trust in Allah and

immediately after one of the five daily prayers, for the Prophet at his Farewell Pilgrimage assumed *ihram* after the *Zuhr* prayer. However, if it is not the time of any obligatory prayer, one may pray two *rak'ahs* of voluntary prayer and then make one's intention known for *ihram*.

The female pilgrims who are in their menstruation period should also take a bath, put on their usual clothes and make known their intention for *ihram* and then call out *talbiyah*. However, for performing hajj or umrah rites, they will wait till their menstruation period is over and then take the bath of purification.

Once a pilgrim has entered into the state of *ihram*, he is then obliged to complete the hajj or umrah. If, however, he is sick or fears some kind of obstruction, he can include the following condition in his intention of *ihram*:

> "If I am obstructed on the journey, then I will be released from *ihram* wherever Allah obstructs me."

In such case, if he is prevented from completing his hajj, no ransom will be due from him.

become good and pure and loving towards others.

In ihram the men and women of all countries, all races and all stations in life look alike. No one can then take pride of place over another. After all, in the eyes of God, all men are equal.

Whether a person is rich or poor, black or white, handsome or plain, fast or slow, famous or unknown, clever or ordinary – is not important – what matters is the sincerity of his striving for goodness and his faith in God.

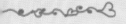

Ihram Garments for Men

The *ihram* garment for men consists of two seamless pieces of cloth, one worn around the waist and the other thrown loosely over the shoulder. The head should be left uncovered. Preferably, these wrappings should be white in colour. But if white is not available, coloured wrappings may be used, provided that they are not of too brighter colour. It does not matter whether they are of cotton or woolen material.

Ihram Garments for Women

There is no particular *ihram* garment for women. They can wear clothes of their own choice, provided they are not attractive in outward appearance. They should cover the whole body except for the face and hands. The face and hands should remain exposed. In the state of *ihram* women are prohibited from wearing gloves and tightly-fitted face covers. The women pilgrims should not use scent.

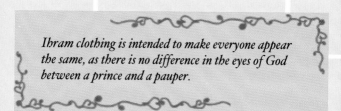

Ihram clothing is intended to make everyone appear the same, as there is no difference in the eyes of God between a prince and a pauper.

Prohibitions in the State of Ihram

The following are the acts which are prohibited for pilgrims while in the state of *ihram*.

- Shaving the head or cutting the hair

- Cutting nails

- Hunting of animals (catching fishes is allowed)

- Helping a hunter by pointing out game to him.

- Indecent or obscene speech

- Disputing or quarelling with others

- Sexual intercourse

- Acts of disobedience to God

- Marrying (also sending a proposal of marriage or arranging marriages for others)

- Applying perfume

- Covering the head (for men only)

- Wearing stitched clothes and shoes (for men only)

- Wearing gloves (for women only)

- Covering the face with tight-fitted wrappings (for women only)

If a pilgrim fails to complete his/her hajj or umrah after entering into the state of *ihram* or commits an act which is forbidden in the state of *ihram*, he/she shall have to compensate for this by fasting for three days, or feeding six poor people or sacrificing an animal.

Engaging in sexual intercourse during the state of *ihram* is not allowed, but there is no compensation to be made for this. Rather, in such a case the hajj or umrah will be invalid and the offenders shall have to repeat it if it is an obligatory hajj. Similarly, there is no fine for disobeying God's commandments or using obscene or abusive language. In such cases, though the offender's hajj or umrah will not be nullified. However, he/she should be sincere in his/her repentance to God, imploring Him for His forgiveness for the sin he/she has committed.

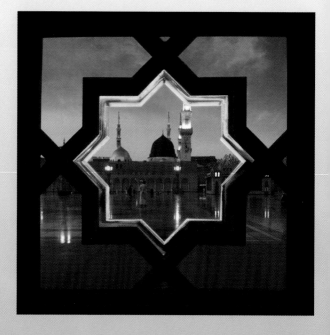

Calling out the Talbiya

After assuming *ihram* the pilgrim should begin to call out *talbiyah*. The wording is as follows:

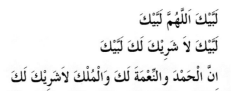

$$\text{لَبَّيْكَ اَللَّهُمَّ لَبَّيْكَ}$$

$$\text{لَبَّيْكَ لاَ شَرِيْكَ لَكَ لَبَّيْكَ}$$

$$\text{اِنَّ الْحَمْدَ وَالنِّعْمَةَ لَكَ وَالْمُلْكَ لاَشَرِيْكَ لَكَ}$$

Here I am, O Allah, here I am.

Here I am, You have no partner. Here I am.

Surely, all praise and favour is Yours and sovereignty. You have no partner.

On the occasion of his Farewell Pilgrimage, the Prophet, upon reaching Dhul-Hulayfa, offered the *Zuhr* prayer, assumed *ihram*, mounted his she-camel and then began to call out the *talbiyah*.

Throughout the state of *ihram* the male pilgrims should pronounce the words of the *talbiyah* in a loud voice, particularly after obligatory prayers and upon passing the carvans while the female pilgrims should pronounce it in a low and soft voice. It was also the practice of the Prophet to call out *"Allahu Akbar"* three times on reaching any hill. For hajj the *talbiyah* begins with the assumption of the *ihram* and comes to an end with the throwing of the first pebble on the 10th of Dhul-Hijjah, whereas umrah begins with *ihram* and ends with the commencement of *tawaf*.

> *Talbiyah, or the often repeated labbaika prayer, is a believer's response to God's call. This is a foretaste of the Day of Judgment, when "the trumpet will be blown and behold, they will rise up from their graves and hasten to their Lord." (36:51)*

Tawaf al-Qudum or Tawaf of Arrival

On reaching al-Masjid al-Haram the pilgrims should stop calling out *talbiyah* in the case of umrah and in case of hajj, they should stop calling out *talbiyah* with the throwing of the first pebble on the 10th of Dhul-Hijjah. Then they should first kiss the Black Stone. If, due to overcrowding, it is not possible to kiss it, they may touch it with their hands or with a stick and then kiss it later. If even this

is not possible, then it will suffice merely to point towards it with their hands or a stick. But in this case, the hands or stick should not be kissed. And then, with the Kabah to their left, they should start circling it. They should make seven rounds of the Kabah, the first three rounds at a brisk pace and the remaining four rounds at a slower pace. While performing *tawaf,* the pilgrims should keep their right arms and shoulders bare and the left shoulders covered with the wrapping of *ihram.* However, this will not apply to the women pilgrims. In each of the seven rounds, upon reaching the Black Stone, the pilgrims should say *"Allahu Akbar".*

While performing the *tawaf,* as one passes al-Rukn al-Yamani heading towards the Black Stone, one should recite the following *dua:*

رَبَّنَا آتِنَا فِي الدُّنْيَا حَسَنَةً وَفِي الآخِرَةِ حَسَنَةً وَّقِنَا عَذَابَ النَّارِ

> Our Lord, grant us good in this world as well as good in the world to come, and protect us from the torment of the Fire.

The kissing of al-Rukn al-Yamani not having been laid down by the Prophet, one should rather touch it with the hand or with a stick. If this is not possible, one should pass by it without pointing towards it. Besides the above *dua,* the Prophet has not been quoted as reciting any other particular supplication during *tawaf.* Hence, the pilgrims may recite any supplication of their own choice.

It is better to perform *tawaf* near the walls of the Kabah, but if this is not possible due to huge crowds of people, then longer circuits should be made to avoid pushing and causing inconvenience to others. This *tawaf* performed upon arriving at Makkah is known as *tawaf al qudum* (or *tawaf* of arrival).

Tawaf *or going around the Kabah, means revolving forever around our Lord, like the planets around the sun. Our Creator looks after us all our lives, so we must obey and be constantly aware of Him; we must avoid things He has banned and do good works that please Him and remember Him "when standing, sitting and lying down, and reflect on the creation of the heavens and the earth." (Al-'Imran 3:190-191)*

The Station of Abraham

Upon completion of *tawaf al qudum,* the pilgrims should proceed to Maqam Ibrahim (Station of Abraham) reciting the following verse of the Quran:

وَاتَّخِذُوا مِنْ مَقَامِ اِبْراهِيْمَ مُصلَّى

"Make the place where Abraham stood a place of worship."

Then they should offer two *rak'ahs* behind Maqam Ibrahim, reciting surah al-Kafirun in the first *rak'ah* and surah al-Ikhlas in the second. If Maqam Ibrahim is overcrowded, one may offer them at any other place in al-Masjid al-Haram or even outside it. After performing these two *rak'ahs* of *tawaf,* they should return to the Kabah and kiss the Black Stone.

Then the pilgrims should go to the Well of Zamzam and drink its water and pour it over their heads. In fact, Zamzam water is a great blessing of Allah. It confers both blessing and healing.

Regarding its water the Prophet once said:

"Zamzam water is for whatever one drinks it for."

He also said:

"It satisfies as food and cures illness."

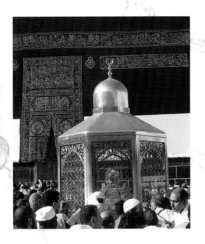

After drinking its water, one should recite this *dua*:

اَللّٰهُمَّ اِنّي أَسْأَلُكَ عِلْمًا نَافِعًا ورِزْقاً وَاسِعاً وَشِفَاءَ مِنْ كُلِّ دَاءٍ

"O Allah, I ask of You beneficial knowledge, abundant provision, and a cure for all diseases."

Zamzam, the spring which gushed forth by God's will, saving the lives of Hajar and her baby Ismail, shows that trusting believers will be duly rewarded by Allah, perhaps even by a miracle. As this water quenches the thirst of millions of pilgrims year after year, without its flow ever stopping, it signals God's immense power and His love for His creatures.

Sa'i or Brisk Walk

Next, the pilgrims should perform *sa'i* (brisk walk) between Safa and Marwah, starting from Safa and finishing at Marwah. When first ascending Mount Safa, they should say:

إنَّ الصَّفَا والْمَرْوَةَ مِنْ شَعَائِرِ اللهِ اَبْدَأُ بِمَا بَدَأَ اللهُ به

"Safa and Marwah are among the symbols set up by God.
I begin with that with which Allah began."

They should ascend Safa until they can see the Kabah and face it and then they should declare God's unity and His greatness saying:

"Allahu Akbar" and *"La ilaha illallahu."*

And then they should recite the following *dua* three times followed by other *duas* of their own:

لاَ اِلَهَ اِلاَّ اللهُ وَحْدَهُ لاَشَرِيكَ لَهُ، لَهُ الْمُلْكُ وَلَـهُ
الْحَمْدُ وَهُوَ عَلَى كُلِّ شَيْئٍ قَـدِيرٍ، لاَ اِلَــهَ الاَّ اللهُ
وَحْدَهُ اَنْجَزَ وَعْدَهُ وَنَصَرَ عَبْدَهُ وَهَـزَمَ الْاَحْـزَابَ
وَحْدَهُ.

"There is no deity but Allah alone, He has no partner.
Sovereignty is His, and praise is His and He has power over all
things. There is no deity but Allah alone. He fulfilled His
promise and helped His servant and defeated the parties
alone."

34

Afterwards, they should descend from Safa and walk towards Marwah, hastening between the two green markers. Upon climbing Mount Marwah and facing the Kabah, they should recite those supplications they recited on Safa. In this way they should complete seven one-way trips between Safa and Marwah, repeating the aforesaid supplications at each trip and finishing at Marwah.

After completing the *sa'i* those pilgrims who have announced their intention to perform hajj *tamattu'* should remove their *ihram* garments and shave their heads or cut their hair. Here umrah is complete. Pilgrims performing this type of hajj will put on their *ihram* for hajj on 8th Dhul-Hijjah again and express their intention in their hearts to perform hajj.

> *Sa'i or walking briskly between the Safa and Marwah Hills, recalls the great struggle of Ibrahim's wife, Hajar, and her total trust in Allah throughout. Doing as Hajar did some 4000 years ago shows believers how they must "run for God" if necessary.*

Departure for Mina

On the 8th day of Dhul-Hijjah, calling out *talbiyah* loudly, the pilgrims should proceed to Mina and stay there for the whole day and night. They should not leave Mina until the morning of the 9th of Dhul-Hijjah when the sun rises. During their stay at Mina they should shorten their prayers.

Departure for Arafat

On the 9th day of Dhul-Hijjah after sunrise, the pilgrims should set out for Arafat, calling out *takbir* and *talbiyah*. They should preferably make a stop at Namirah on the outskirts of the Valley of Arafat and listen to the sermon delivered by the Imam. They should then offer the *Zuhr* and *Asr* prayers, shortening and combining them and saying only one *adhan* and two *iqamahs*.

On the occasion of the Farewell Pilgrimage when the Prophet had delivered his sermon on the plain of Arafat, Bilal called the *adhan*. The Prophet led the *Zuhr* prayer, shortening it to two *rak'ahs*. Immediately afterwards Bilal again called *iqamah* and the Prophet led the *Asr* prayer, performing, again only two *rak'ahs*.

After offering these prayers, the pilgrims

should enter the plain of Arafat and, facing the *qiblah* and raising their hands, they should continue to make supplications until sunset. During their supplication they should also call out *talbiyah*. The Prophet has said:

> "The best supplication is that of the day of Arafat"

He further said:

> "On no other day does Allah set free as many of his servants from the Fire as on the day of Arafat. On that day He is face to face with His servants and is proud of the pilgrims before the angels and asks them what it is they want."

Assembling at Arafat is, for the pilgrims, like standing before God on the Day of Judgement. The Quran says, "When the trumpet is blown, behold, from the graves they rush forth to their Lord" (Ya Sin, 36:51). And indeed, thousands and thousands of God's servants flock in from all sides to witness the event, taking no pride in colour, creed or position, all dressed in the same, simple attire and recite the same words of the talbiyah.

Muzdalifa, where pilgrims stay overnight, reminds the pilgrims of the homeless and the needy, as their lifestyle in small tents has to be very simple.

Leaving for Muzdalifah

After sunset on this day, the pilgrims should leave Arafat for Muzdalifah without offering the *Maghrib* prayer. It is not permissible to depart before sunset. Upon reaching Muzdalifah, they should offer both the *Maghrib* and *Isha* prayers together with the recitation of one *adhan* and two *iqamahs*. The *Isha* prayer should be shortened to two *rak'ahs*. No *sunnah* or voluntary prayers should be offered on this night.

The pilgrims will pass the night at Muzdalifah and, after offering the *Fajr* prayer, they will proceed to al-Mash'ar al-Haram and then, facing the *qiblah,* they should make their supplications to Allah and remember Him until daylight.

It should be noted that it is not essential for every pilgrim to stand near the mosque of Muzdalifah, as the Prophet said:

> "I am standing here but the whole of Muzdalifah is a standing place."

If anyone has women or children or any sick person with him, he can send them to Mina at night.

When it is daylight, the pilgrims should proceed to Mina before sunrise. On the way to Mina, they should pick up seven small, pea-size pebbles. They should keep in mind that there is no fixed place for picking up pebbles. When they arrive at the Valley of Muhassir, they should hasten through it, avoiding picking up pebbles there.

The Day of Sacrifice

On the 10th of Dhul-Hijjah, upon reaching Mina and after sunrise, they should throw seven pebbles at al-Jamarah al-Aqabah (the largest Jamarah) saying '*Allahu Akbar*' each time. While throwing pebbles they should stop reciting the *talbiyah*. Those who cannot perform *ramy* (throwing of the pebbles) before noon due to overcrowding are allowed to do so in the afternoon.

After stoning the greatest Jamarah, the pilgrims should slaughter their sacrificial animal at any convenient place in Mina or even in Makkah. The Prophet said:

> "I slaughtered here, but the whole of Mina is a place of slaughtering."

It is preferable to offer the sacrifice on the 10th of Dhul-Hijjah. However, one can do it on any one of the following three days, which are known as "days of *tashreeq*". A pilgrim who cannot afford to offer a whole animal in sacrifice can share the sacrifice of an animal like a camel or a cow. A goat or a sheep cannot be shared.

It is essential for every pilgrim performing the *qiran* or *tamattu‘* type of hajj to sacrifice an animal. However, one who does not have sufficient means to offer the sacrifice must observe ten days of fasting— three days during hajj and seven days upon returning home. At the time of slaughtering the animal, one should say *"Bismillah Allahu Akbar"*.

Next, they should either shave their heads or trim their hair. It is desirable for those (male) pilgrims who are performing the *tamattu‘* type of hajj to shorten their hair on performing umrah and then shave their heads on the 10th day of Dhul-Hijjah. Women are forbidden to shave their heads. They should only cut the ends of their hair. The pilgrims should now remove their *ihrams*. This is the point when all restrictions of the state of *ihram* are lifted except that of conjugal relationships. After these devotional acts of this Day of Sacrifice, the pilgrims should go to Makkah for the *tawaf* which is known as *tawaf ifadah*. This *tawaf* is an essential part of hajj. Unlike *tawaf qudum*, in this *tawaf* observing *raml* (brisk walk) and *idhtiba* (slow walk) is not required.

The Feast of Sacrifice reminds believers of the readiness of the Prophet Ibrahim to give up his most beloved son. Likewise, on this day believers reaffirm their belief in Allah and pledge themselves to parting with their precious belongings, if there is a need for it. The Quran describes these sentiments in the following verse: "Truly, my prayers, my sacrifice, my life and my death all belong to Allah, the Lord of the Worlds." (Al-An'am, 6:162)

After the *tawaf* they should offer two *rak'ah* prayer and then drink Zamzam water and pour it on their heads as well. If a pilgrim is performing the *tamattu'* type of hajj, he should perform *sa'i* for the second time between Safa and Marwah after the *tawaf*. However those performing hajj *qiran* or *ifrad* will do only one *sa'i*.

If anyone, for a valid reason cannot perform the *sa'i* on this day, he can do it on any day during *ayyam tashreeq*. After performing this *sa'i*, the pilgrims become free of all restrictions of the state of *ihram* including sexual intercourse. Now they should again return to Mina and stay there at night.

The pilgrims can stay in Mina either until the 12th or 13th day of Dhul Hijjah, throwing pebbles each day. However, those pilgrims who intend to leave Mina on the 12th of Dhul-Hijjah should do so before sunset after throwing the pebbles of that day.

These three days, 11th, 12th and 13th of Dhul Hijjah, are called *ayyam at-tashreeq*. Apart from *ramy* (stoning the Jamarahs), the pilgrims should be engaged in supplicating and remembering Allah during these days. They can also meet with fellow pilgrims and rejoice. Regarding these days, the Prophet said:

> "The days of *tashreeq* are the days of rejoicing and remembering Allah."

The Manner of Ramy, or Stoning the Jamarahs, on the Days of Tashreeq

After the decline of the sun at noon, the pilgrims should throw seven pebbles at al-Jamarah al-Sughra (the small Jamarah), seven at al-Jamarah al-Wusta (the middle Jamarah) and seven at al-Jamarah al-Aqabah (the largest Jamarah) saying *'Allahu Akbar'* upon throwing each pebble. After performing the *ramy* of these Jamarahs, they should move a little ahead, stand facing the Kabah and make supplication. Supplication should not be made after throwing pebbles on the largest Jamarah.

Ramy, *or throwing pebbles at Satan's pillars at Mina, shows how believers must avoid temptation. Whenever their inner "satan" tempts them to err, they will mentally "throw pebbles" at it to drive it away.*

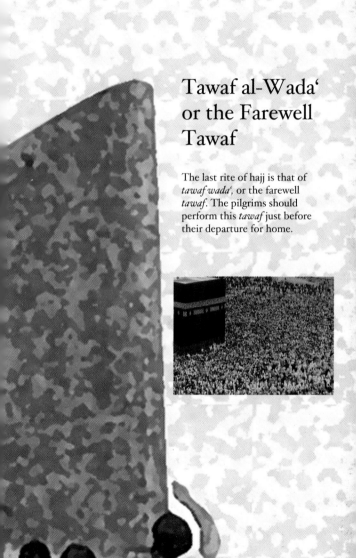

Tawaf al-Wada' or the Farewell Tawaf

The last rite of hajj is that of *tawaf wada'*, or the farewell *tawaf*. The pilgrims should perform this *tawaf* just before their departure for home.

Hajj: Round up

- Upon reaching the *miqat* the pilgrims should put on the *ihram* garments and then form the intention of performing hajj only in the case of hajj *Ifrad* or of performing only umrah in the case of hajj *Tamattu'* or umrah and hajj both in the case of hajj *Qiran*. And then they should begin calling out the *talbiyah* and should continue doing so intermittently.

- On reaching Makkah, they should enter al Masjid al Haram and perform *tawaf al qudum*. They should observe *raml* and *idhtiba* in this *tawaf*. In each circuit they should kiss the Black Stone if possible, otherwise touch it with their hands or a stick and then kiss it. If it is too crowded, they should merely point toward it with the hand saying *Allahu Akbar* each time. During *tawaf*, they may recite any proper *dua* they wish. However, between al Rukn al Yamani and the Black Stone, it is preferable to recite:

رَبَّنَا آتِنَا فِي الدُّنْيَا حَسَنَةً وَّ فِي الآخِرَةِ حَسَنَةً وَّقِنَا عَذَابَ النَّارِ

- After performing *tawaf qudum*, the pilgrims should proceed to the Maqam Ibrahim reciting وَاتَّخِذُوا مِنْ مَقَامِ إِبْرَاهِيْمَ مُصَلَّى then pray two *rak'ah* behind it if possible. If it is too crowded, they should offer this prayer anywhere else.

- Then they should go to the Well of Zamzam, drink their fill of its water and pour it on their heads.

- Then they should go back to the Black Stone and either kiss it or touch it with their hand or a stick.

"إنَّ الصَّفَا والمروةَ من شَعَائِرِ اللهِ" أبدأ بما بدأ اللهُ به.

- Then they should perform *sa'i* between Safa and Marwah, starting from Safa and finishing at Marwah. When first ascending the mount of Safa, they should recite

After having ascended Safa and seen the Kabah, they should face the *qibla* and recite the *dua* mentioned in the book three times. Afterwards, they should descend and proceed towards Marwah. Upon ascending Marwah and facing the *qiblah*, they should recite the same *dua* as they recited on Safa. In this way, they should complete seven one-way trips, finishing at Marwah.

- After completing the *sa'i* they should either cut their hair or shave their heads and take off *ihram* garments. At this point the umrah

is completed. They should then wait until the 8th of Dhul Hijjah for the hajj rites to begin.

- On the 8th of Dhul Hijjah, the pilgrims should put on the *ihram* garments and announce their intention to perform hajj, saying *"Labbayka bi hajjin"*.

- Calling out the *talbiyah*, they should proceed to Mina either on foot or by transport and stay there for the whole day and night. They should shorten their *Zuhr, Asr* and *Isha* prayers.

- On the 9th of Dhul Hijjah, after sunrise, they should set out for Arafat, calling out the *talbiyah*. At Namirah which is situated on the outskirts of the plain of Arafat, the pilgrims should make a stop. Then they should enter the plain of Arafat and, facing the *qiblah*, make their supplications until sunset.

45

- After sunset, without offering the *Maghrib* prayer, the pilgrims should leave Arafat for Muzdalifah. On reaching there, they should offer the *Maghrib* and *Isha* prayers together. They should pass the night in Muzdalifah.

- After the *Fajr* prayer, they should proceed to al Mash'ar al Haram and, facing the *qibla,* should supplicate Allah and declare His glory and greatness until the sun has fully risen. They should leave Muzdalifa for Mina before sunrise. On the way to Mina, they should pick up seven pebbles for the first stoning and then go directly to the largest Jamarah.

- On the 10th Dhul Hijjah, after sunrise they should throw these seven pebbles picked up by them on the way to Mina at this greatest Jamarah, saying '*Allahu Akbar*' at each throwing.

- They should then slaughter the sacrificial animal, preferably with their own hands.

- Afterwards, the pilgrims should shave their heads or cut their hair short.

- Now they are free to take off their *ihram* garments. All restrictions of the state of *ihram* are lifted, except that of having marital relations.

After taking off the *ihram* garments, they should go to Makka for *tawaf ifadah,* followed by two *rak'ahs* of prayer, the drinking of

Zamzam water and the pouring of it on their heads. After the *tawaf*, they should perform *sa'i* between Safa and Marwah. At this point all restrictions of the state of *ihram*, including that of having marital relations are lifted. Now they should return to Mina and spend the night there.

- On the 11th day of Dhul Hijjah after the sun declines at noon, the pilgrims should throw seven pebbles at the small Jamarah, saying *Allahu Akbar* at each throwing. Then they should stand facing the *qiblah* and supplicate Allah. Then they should go to the middle Jamarah, throw seven pebbles, and supplicate in the same manner as they did at the small Jamarah. Lastly, they should go to the large Jamarah and throw seven pebbles. They should not supplicate after stoning this Jamarah.

- On the 12th day of Dhul Hijjah after the sun declines at noon, the pilgrims should throw seven pebbles at each of the three Jamarahs in the same manner as they did the previous day. If a pilgrim intends to leave Mina on this day, he should leave after throwing the pebbles and before the sun sets.

- Those pilgrims who stay on at Mina until the 13th day of Dhul Hijjah should throw seven pebbles at each of the three Jamarahs in the same manner as they did on the first two days. These three days are known as *ayyam at tashreeq*. During these days the pilgrims should slaughter as many animals as they can, eat their meat and distribute whatever is surplus.

- The last rite of hajj is that of *tawaf al wada'*. *Wada* means farewell. This *tawaf* should be performed just before departing for home.

A Visit to the City of Madinah

Madinah is the city to which the Prophet migrated after being persecuted by the polytheists of Makkah. Visiting the city of Madinah is not an essential part of hajj, nor does it bear any relation to hajj. However, many historical sites are located there. And, above all, the Prophet's grave and his mosque are situated there. About his mosque the Prophet said:

> "A prayer in my mosque is better than one thousand prayers offered in any other mosque, except al Masjid al Haram."

And in this mosque of the Prophet there is a place about which he has said:

> "Between my house and my pulpit there is a garden from the gardens of paradise."

That is why the pilgrims who go to Makkah to perform hajj have an earnest desire to visit the city of Madinah.

Those who visit the city of Madinah should enter the mosque of the Prophet by reciting the same *dua* they recite while entering any other mosque and try to offer two *rak'ah tahiyyatul masjid* prayers in the place between his house and the pulpit. However, if it is too crowded, they should offer them anywhere in the mosque.

After offering those two *rak'ahs*, they should proceed to visit the graves of the Prophet and his two companions, Abu Bakr and Umar.

Standing near the grave of the Prophet they should say:

السّلامُ عليكم يا رسول الله ورحمة الله وبركاته

"Peace be upon you, O messenger of Allah, and Allah's mercy and His blessing."

And near the grave of Abu Bakr they should say:

السلام عليك يا أبابكر

"Peace be on you, O Abu Bakr."

And near the grave of Umar they should say:

السلام عليك يا عمر

"Peace be on you, O Umar."

It should be noted that there is no religious excellence in visiting other mosques or historical sites in Madinah except the mosque of the Prophet and Mosque of Quba. Regarding the Quba Mosque we find a *hadith* of the Prophet in which he says:

"Whoever performs ablution at home and then goes to Quba Mosque, desiring nothing but prayer, gets the reward equal to an umrah."

However, one may visit the other mosques and historical sites of the city without considering it an act of worship.

Hajj on behalf of the Deceased or a Sick Person

If a man who had the ability to perform hajj dies without performing it, his hajj can be performed by his heirs or those whom they nominate to undertake it on his behalf. The expenditure on the hajj journey will be taken out of the deceased's property. This also includes one who had made a vow to perform hajj.

This is supported by a *hadith* related by Abdullah bin Abbas, He says:

> "A lady asked the Prophet, "My mother made a vow to perform hajj, but she died before she performed it. Should I perform hajj on her behalf?" The Prophet replied, "Yes, perform hajj for her."

Likewise, a man for whom hajj is obligatory but, due to old age or illness cannot perform it, must send someone to perform hajj on his behalf. It should be kept in mind that anyone who is going to perform hajj on his behalf must have previously performed his own hajj. On the occasion of the Farewell Pilgrimage the Prophet heard a man calling out the *talbiyah* on behalf of Shubrumah. He asked that person whether he had performed his own hajj. He replied in the negative. On hearing this, the Prophet ordered him to perform hajj for himself first and then on behalf of Shubrumah. The person peforming hajj on behalf of another person will get the reward of a voluntary hajj.

The Prayers of Hajj

- *Dua* on boarding the conveyance:

سُبْحَانَ الَّذِي سَخَّرَ لَنَا هَذَا وَمَا كُنَّا لَهُ مُقْرِنِيْنَ وَإِنَّا
إِلَى رَبِّنَا لَمُنْقَلِبُوْنَ. اللّٰهُمَّ هَوِّنْ عَلَيْنَا هَــذَا الــسَّفَرَ
وَاطْوِعَنَّا بُعْدَهُ اللّٰهُمَّ اَنْتَ الصَّاحِبُ فِــي الــسَّفَرِ
وَالْخَلِيْفَةُ فِي الْأَهْلِ، اللّٰهُمَّ اِنِّي اَعُوذُ بِكَ مِنْ وَعْثَاء
السَّفَرِ وَكَآبَةِ الْمَنْظَرِ وَسُوءِ الْمُنْقَلَبِ فِــي الْمَــالِ
وَالْأَهْلِ.

Glory be to Him who has subjected this for us though we were
unable to subdue it. Behold, we are assuredly to return to our
Lord. O Allah, make this journey easy for us and roll up its
distance from us. O Allah, You are my companion on the
journey and protector in my home. O Allah, I seek Your
protection against the evils I may encounter during this
journey, and the undesirable things I may see and that I should
make an evil return to my belongings, wife and children.

52

- *Dua* during the journey

اللهم رب السَّمَوات السَّبْعِ وَمَا اَظْلَلْنَ، وربُّ الأرْضِينَ السَّبْعِ وَمَا اَقْلَلْنَ، وربُّ الشَّيَاطِينِ وَمَا اَضْلَلْنَ، وربُّ الرِّيَاحِ وَمَا ذَرَيْنَ، اَسْأَلُكَ خَيْرَ هَذِهِ الْقَرْيَةِ، وَخَيْرَ اَهْلِهَا وَخَيْرَ مَا فِيهَا، وَاَعُوذُ بِكَ مِنْ شَرِّهَا وَشَرِّ اَهْلِهَا وَشَرِّ مَا فِيهَا.

O Allah, Lord of the seven heavens and all that they cover,
Lord of the seven earths and that which they carry, Lord of
the devils and those lead astray, and Lord of the winds and
that which they scatter, I ask of You the good of this town
and the good of its people and the good in it. And I seek
refuge in You from its evil and from the evil of its people and
from the evil of that which is in it.

- *Dua* at a stopover

اَعُوذُ بِكَلِمَاتِ اللهِ التَّامَّاتِ مِنْ شَرِّ مَا خَلَقَ

I seek refuge with the perfect words of Allah from the evil of
that which He created.

- *Dua* at the time of assuming *ihram* and afterwards (*Talbiyah*)

لَبَّيْكَ اللّهُمَّ لَبَّيْكَ لَبَّيْكَ لاَ شَرِيكَ لَكَ لَبَّيْكَ. إِنَّ الْحَمْدَ وَالنِّعْمَةَ لَكَ وَالْمُلْكَ لاَشَرِيْكَ لَكَ

I am here, O Allah, I am here. I am here, You have no partner,
I am here. All praise and favour is Yours and sovereignty. You
have no partner.

- *Dua* upon entering Makkah

لاَ إِلَهَ إِلاَّ الله وَحْدَهُ لاَ شَرِيْكَ لَهُ، لَهُ الْمُلْكُ وَلَـهُ
الْحَمْدُ، وَهُوَ عَلَى كُلِّ شَيْءٍ قَدِيْرٌ.

There is no god but Allah. He is alone. He has no partner.
Sovereignty is His and praise is His. And He has power over all
things.

- *Dua* when entering al Masjid al Haram

بِسْمِ الله وَالصَّلاَةُ وَالسَّلاَمُ عَلَى رَسُوْلِ الله، اللّهُـمَّ
افْتَحْ لِي أَبْوَابَ رَحْمَتِكَ.

In the name of Allah, peace and blessings be upon the
Messenger of Allah. O Allah, open the doors of Your mercy
for me.

- *Dua* during the *tawaf*

رَبَّنَا آتِنَا فِى الدُّنْيَا حَسَنَةً وَّ فِي الآخِرَةِ حَسَنَةً وَّقِنَـا
عَذَابَ النَّارِ.

Our Lord, grant us good in this world as well as good in the
world to come, and protect us from the torment of the Fire.

- *Dua* while proceeding to Maqam Ibrahim

وَاتَّخِذُوا مِنْ مَقَامِ إِبْرَاهِيْمَ مُصَلَّى

And make the station of Abraham a place of worship.

- *Dua* after drinking Zamzam water

اللّٰهُمَّ اِنِّي أَسْأَلُكَ عِلْمًا نَافِعًا وَرِزْقًا وَاسِعًا وَشِـفَاءً
مِنْ كُلِّ دَاءٍ

O Allah, I ask of You beneficial knowledge, extensive sustenance and a cure for all diseases.

- *Dua* before beginning *sa'i*

إِنَّ الصَّفَا وَالْمَرْوَةَ مِنْ شَعَائِرِ اللهِ، أَبْدَأُ بِمَا بَدَأَ اللهُ بِهِ

Surely, Safa and Marwah are symbols of Allah. I begin with what Allah began.

- *Dua* after ascending the mount

لَا إِلَهَ إِلَّا اللهُ اللهُ أَكْبَرُ

There is no god but Allah. Allah is great.

لاَ إِلَهَ إِلاَّ اللهُ وَحْدَهُ لاَ شَرِيكَ لَهُ، لَهُ الْمُلْكُ وَلَـهُ الْحَمْدُ وَهُوَ عَلَى كُلِّ شَيئٍ قَـدِيْرٌ، لاَ اِلَـهَ اِلاَّ اللهُ وَحْدَهُ اَنْجَزَ وَعْدَهُ وَنَصَرَ عَبْدَهُ وَهَـزَمَ الأحْـزَابَ وَحْدَهُ.

There is no god but Allah, who is alone. He has no partner. His is sovereignty and His is praise. And He has power over all things. There is no god but Allah, the one and only, who fulfilled His promise and helped His servants and defeated the confederates alone.

- *Dua* to be recited between Safa and Marwa

رَبِّ اغْفِرْلِي وَارْحَمْ وَاَنْتَ الأَعَزُّ الأكْرَمُ

My Lord, forgive and have mercy, for You are the Mighty, the Honorable One.

- *Dua* on the day of Arafat

لاَ إِلَهَ إِلاَّ اللهُ وَحْدَهُ لاَ شَرِيكَ لَهُ، لَهُ الْمُلْكُ وَلَـهُ الْحَمْدُ وَهُوَ عَلَى كُلِّ شَيئٍ قَدِيْرٌ.

"There is no god but Allah, the one and only. He has no partner. His is the kingdom and His is praise. And He has power over all things."

One should recite other *duas* also from the Quran and the Hadith. The supplication of this day has great importance. The Prophet said:

"On no other day does Allah set free as many of His servants from the Fire as He does on the day of Arafat."

- *Dua* at the time of slaughtering the animal

بسم الله الله اَكْبَرُ

In the name of Allah, Allah is the most great.

- *Dua* on visiting the Prophet's grave

السَّلاَمُ عَلَيْكَ يَا رَسُولَ اللهِ وَرَحْمَةُ اللهِ وَبَرَكَاتُهُ

"Peace be upon you, O Messenger of Allah, and Allah's mercy and His blessings."

Some Prayers from the Quran and the Hadith

Note: One can recite these *duas* at any time of one's own choosing.

رَبَّنَا آتِنَا فِي الدُّنْيَا حَسَنَةً وَّ فِي الآخِرَةِ حَسَنَةً وَّقِنَـــا عَذَابَ النَّارِ.

Our Lord, give us good in this world and good in the hereafter and defend us from the torment of the Fire.

رَبَّنَا ظَلَمْنَا اَنْفُسَنَا وَانْ لَّمْ تَغْفِرْ لَنَا وَتَرْحَمْنَا لَنَكُونَنَّ مِنَ الْخَاسِرِيْنَ.

Our Lord, we have wronged our souls; if You do not forgive us and have mercy on us, we shall be among the lost.

رَبَّنَا لاَ تُزِغْ قُلُوبَنَا بَعْدَ إِذْ هَدَيْتَنَا وَهَبْ لَنَا مِنْ لَّدُنْكَ رَحْمَةً اِنَّكَ أَنْتَ الْوَهَّابُ.

Our Lord, let not our hearts deviate after You have guided us but grant us mercy from Your presence; for You are the best grantor (of bounties).

رَبَّنَا لاَ تُؤَاخِذْنَا اِنْ نَسِيْنَا أَوْ اَخْطَأْنَا، رَبَّنَا وَلاَ تَحْمِـــلْ عَلَيْنَا اصْراً كَمَا حَمَلْتَهُ عَلَى الَّذِينَ مِنْ قَبْلِنَا، رَبَّنَا وَلاَ تُحَمِّلْنَا مَا لاَ طَاقَةَ لَنَا بِهِ، وَاعْفُ عَنَّـــا وَاغْفِـــرْ لَنَـــا وَارْحَمْنَا أَنْتَ مَوْلاَنَا فَانْصُرْنَا عَلَى الْقَوْمِ الْكَافِرِينَ.

Our Lord, do not take us to task if we forget or make a mistake! Our Lord, do not place on us a burden like the one You placed on those before us! Our Lord, do not place on us a burden we have not the strength to bear! Pardon us; and forgive us; and have mercy on us. You are our Lord and Sustainer, so help us against those who deny the truth.

رَبِّ اغْفِرْلِي وَلِوَالِدَيَّ وَلِمَنْ دَخَـــلَ بَيْتِــيَ مُؤْمِنًـــا وَلِلْمُؤْمِنِينَ وَالْمُؤْمِنَات وَلاَ تَزِدِ الظَّالِمِينَ الاَّ تَبَاراً.

My Lord! Forgive me and my parents and every true believer who enters my house, forgive all the believing men and believing women; and bring down nothing but destruction upon the unjust.

رَبِّ أَوْزِعْنِي اَنْ اَشْكُرَ نِعْمَتَكَ الَّتِي اَنْعَمْتَ عَلَــيَّ وَعَلَى وَالِدَيَّ وَاَنْ اَعْمَلَ صَالِحاً تَرْضَاه وَاَصْلِحْ لِي فِي ذُرِّيَّتِي اِنِّي تُبْتُ إِلَيْكَ وَاِنِّي مِنَ الْمُسْلِمِينَ.

O my Lord! Help me to be grateful for Your favours which You have bestowed upon me, and upon both my parents, and to do good deeds that will please You. Grant me good descendants. Truly, I have turned to You and, truly, I submit to You.

لاَ اَلَهَ إلاَّ أَنْتَ سُبْحَانَكَ إِنِّي كُنْتُ مِنَ الظَّالِمِينَ.

There is no god but You. Glory be to You, certainly I am of those who have wronged themselves.

اللَّهُمَّ اغْفِرْلِي خَطِيئَتِي وَجَهْلِي واسْرَافِي فِي اَمْـرِي وَمَا أَنْتَ اَعْلَمُ بِهِ مِنِّي. اللَّهُمَّ اغْفِرْلِي هَزْلِي وَجِدِّي وَخَطَائِي وَعَمْدِي وَكُلُّ ذَلِكَ عَنْدِي. اللَّهُمَّ اغْفِرْلِي مَاقَدَّمْتُ وَمَا أَخَّرْتُ وَمَا اَسْرَرْتُ وَمَا اَعْلَنْتُ وَمَـا أَنْتَ اَعْلَمُ بِهِ مِنِّي، اَنْتَ الْمُقَدِّمُ وَاَنْتَ الْمُؤَخِّرُ وَاَنْتَ عَلَى كُلِّ شَيئٍ قَدِيرٌ.

O Allah, forgive me my sins, my ignorance and my excesses, and that which You know more than me. O Allah, forgive me for whatever I have done in jest or in seriousness, by mistake or after deliberation, and all those who are with me. O Allah, forgive me my past sins and my present sins, and those that I committed secretly or openly and that which You know more than me. You are the Advancer, the Postponer, and You have power over all things.

اللّٰهُمَّ اَنْتَ رَبِّي لاَ اِلَهَ اِلاَّ اَنْتَ، خَلَقْتَنِي وَاَنَا عَبْدُكَ، وَاَنَا عَلَى عَهْدِكَ وَوَعْدِكَ مَا اسْتَطَعْتُ، اَعُوذُ بِكَ مِنْ شَرِّ مَا صَنَعْتُ اَبُوءُ لَكَ بِنِعْمَتِكَ عَلَيَّ وَاَبُوءُ بِـذَنْبِي فَاغْفِرْلِي، فَإِنَّهُ لاَ يَغْفِرُ الذُّنُوبَ إِلاَّ اَنْتَ.

O Allah, You are my Lord. There is no god but You.
You created me and I am your servant, and I uphold
Your covenant and promise as much as I can. I seek
refuge in You from the evil I have done. I
acknowledge to You Your favour to me, and I
acknowledge my sins, so forgive me. Indeed, there is
none who can forgive sins except You.

اللّٰهُمَّ اِنِّي اَعُوذُ بِكَ مِنْ زَوَالِ نِعْمَتِكَ وَتَحَوُّلِ عَافِيَتِكَ وَمِنْ فَجْأَةِ نِقْمَتِكَ وَمِنْ جَمِيعِ سَخَطِكَ.

O Allah! I seek refuge in You from the decline of
Your favours and from the withdrawal of Your
protection and from Your sudden revenge and from
all Your displeasure.

اللَّهُمَّ اِنِّي اَعُوذُ بِكَ مِنَ الْهَمِّ وَالْحَـزَنِ وَالْعَجْـزِ وَالْكَسَلِ وَالْجُبْنِ وَالْبُخْلِ وَاَعُوذُ بِكَ مِنْ غَلَبَةِ الدَّيْنِ وَقَهْرِ الرِّجَالِ.

O Allah, I seek refuge in You from anxiety and grief, from weakness and laziness and cowardliness and parsimony, and I seek refuge in You from the burden of debt and the coercion of others.

اللَّهُمَّ اِنِّي اَعُوذُ بِكَ مِنْ عِلْمٍ لاَ يَنْفَعُ، وَمِنْ قَلْبٍ لاَ يَخْشَعُ وَمِنْ نَفْسٍ لاَتَشْبَعُ وَمِنْ دَعْوَةٍ لاَيُسْتَجَابُ لَهَا.

O Allah, I seek refuge with You from a heart that knows no humility, from a soul that is never satisfied, from the knowledge that is of no use and from a prayer that is not answered.

اللَّهُمَّ اَصْلِحْ لِي دِينِي الَّذِي هُوَ عِصْمَةُ اَمْرِي، وَاصْلِحْ لِي دُنْيَايَ الَّتِي فِيهَا مَعَاشِي، وَاصْلِحْ لِي آخِرَتِي الَّتِي اِلَيْهَا مَعَادِي، وَاجْعَلْ الْحَيَاةَ زِيَادَةً لِي فِي كُلِّ خَيْرٍ، وَاجْعَلِ الْمَوتَ رَاحَةً لِيْ مِنْ كُلِّ شَرٍّ.

O Allah, set right my religion for me, which is the safeguard of my affairs; and set right my world for me in which is my livelihood, set right my next world to which is my ultimate return. Increase all that is good in my life and make death a respite for me from every evil.

اللَّهُمَّ رَحْمَتَكَ اَرْجُو فَلاَ تَكِلْنِي إِلَى نَفْسِي طَرْفَةَ عَيْنٍ، وَاَصْلِحْ لِي شَأْنِي كُلَّهُ، لاَ اِلَهَ إِلاَّ اَنْتَ.

O Allah! For Your mercy do I hope, so leave me not to myself for an instant and set right for me all my affairs. There is no god except You.